YOUR MIND
IS LIKE THE SKY

Bronwen Ballard
Laura Carlin

Frances Lincoln
Children's Books

Your mind is like the sky.
Sometimes it's clear and blue.

Sometimes it's fizzy
and stormy
and black
and crackly.

Often
it's
just
a bit
gray.

Your thoughts are like the clouds.
Nice, white, fluffy cloud thoughts like:

"Look
what I can
do,"

or
"I love to ride my bike,"

or "That was a good day."

And darker, meaner, raincloud thoughts,
like "I'm not good at this,"
or "I'll never get this right,"
or even "I'm useless."

Thoughts come and go for all of us all the time.

Half the time they've been and gone
before you've even really noticed.

The trouble with raincloud thoughts is that they're dark and a bit mysterious. They can make everything else seem dark, too.

Without you even noticing,
they can make you feel angry,
or jumpy, or sad and confused.

So what do we do about rainclouds?

You could go exploring.
Some people go right
inside their raincloud thoughts...

...and rummage around.
They think if they can get right to the bottom of their
raincloud thought, they can figure out how to get rid of it.

The problem is, when you're inside a raincloud, the cloud looks

really, **really, BIG.**

And it's hard to see anything else.

You could try
fighting.

But as you'll know if
you've ever fought a
raincloud, all that happens
is you get a bit wet.

You could pretend the raincloud isn't even there.
You could skip about and laugh and tell
everyone how happy you are.

Sometimes this works and
the raincloud floats off.

But if it's a big, dark raincloud thought,
it's probably best to put on your rain boots.

Or you could try
this clever trick.

When a raincloud thought comes into your head, you say "Oh, it's a raincloud thought." And then you notice all the white fluffy cloud thoughts as well.

You notice the blueness of the sky and the tweeting of the birds. You remember that the raincloud thought is just one thought among hundreds and thousands of your thoughts. And you can just let the raincloud thought float gently away.

The trick is to see the whole sky.
It takes a bit of practice to look
inside your head.

But if you just stop every
now and then, you'll begin
to notice that there are
big, shouting thoughts
and little whispering ones,

fast, racing thoughts,

and gentle
creeping ones...

...and that YOU CAN CHOOSE which thoughts
to pay attention to.

Your mind is like the sky.
It's full of thoughts of different
shapes, sizes and colors.
It's full of AMAZING things.

Notes for grown-up readers

Mindfulness is a way of paying attention to our thoughts, kindly and without judgement. When we are mindful, we begin to notice that although our thoughts often seem like the truth, they are really just thoughts, and we don't always have to follow where they lead. As with any skill, it takes regular practice to make mindfulness a habit, but the rewards are huge; protection from anxiety and depression, improved memory and attention, greater levels of happiness and many more.

We can begin at any time, just by gently noticing our thoughts and feelings. As parents and carers, we can help by talking about what is in our minds (and children seem to find this more natural than we do). Here are some ideas to try with your child if you would like to experiment with being more mindful at home.

1. Every now and then, take a moment to notice what is going on in your head, heart and body.

You can sit down and close your eyes to do this, or you can do it while you are cleaning your teeth or taking a walk—anything which doesn't require too much concentration! All you have to do is notice your thoughts and feelings in a way which is kind and accepting.

Is your mind clear and blue, or stormy and crackly?
Are there lots of thoughts fizzing about in there,
or is it moving slowly?

Have your thoughts been like that all day or have they just changed? Whatever you find is fine. Isn't it amazing how different thoughts can be?

2. Notice any fluffy cloud thoughts.

Humans have evolved to notice the negative more than the positive. This keeps us safe in many ways, but it also means our good thoughts tend to drift off without us even noticing them. This is a shame, because positive feelings aren't just nice, they are good for our health and our relationships.

So when you notice a positive thought, pay attention to it. Where did it come from? How does it make you feel? Watch those feelings travel around your body and let yourself enjoy them.

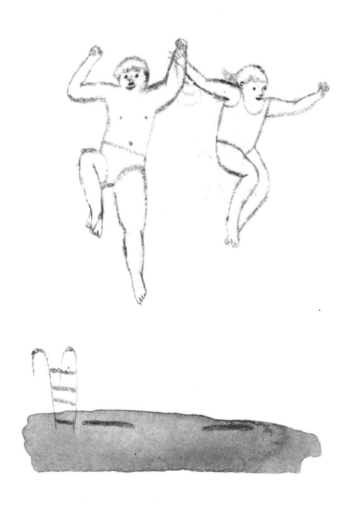

3. Notice any raincloud thoughts.

We all have more difficult thoughts from time to time.
If we try to ignore or "solve" them, they can expand and
become overwhelming. Instead of diving into a raincloud thought,
begin by noticing it is there. Is it a big, dark thought, or just
a small gray one? Have you seen it before, or is it new?
What sort of feelings does it bring with it? Remember
that this thought won't be here forever.

We don't have the power to banish
our children's raincloud thoughts, but
we can let them know that sadness
comes and goes, that they are
stronger than they think, and that,
no matter what, we love them.

For Tilly and Marnie, with my love — B.B.

For Joanna — L.C.

Brimming with creative inspiration, how-to projects, and useful information to enrich your everyday life, Quarto Knows is a favourite destination for those pursuing their interests and passions. Visit our site and dig deeper with our books into your area of interest: Quarto Creates, Quarto Cooks, Quarto Homes, Quarto Lives, Quarto Drives, Quarto Explores, Quarto Gifts, or Quarto Kids.

First Published in 2019 by Frances Lincoln Children's Books, an imprint of The Quarto Group. 400 First Avenue North, Suite 400, Minneapolis MN 55401, USA
www.QuartoKnows.com

ISBN 978-1-78603-986-6

The illustrations were created with coloured pencil, chalk pastel, acrylic and watercolour paint.

Published by Rachel Williams and Jenny Broom
Designed by Zoë Tucker and Karissa Santos
Edited by Kate Davies
Production by Nicolas Zeifman

Manufactured in Shenzhen, China HH092018
9 8 7 6 5 4 3 2 1